101 Question Answers About Dog

Your Best Friend

Dr. N.B. Shridhar
Assistant Professor
Dept. of Pharmacology and Toxicology
Veterinary College, KVAFSU,
Hebbal, Bangalore-560024

Dr. C.S. Arun
1693, 2nd Cross North Aniketana Road
Kuvempunagar, Mysore-23

ibdc publishers
PUBLISHING GREEN

Published by

ibdc publishers
PUBLISHING GREEN

Khushnuma Complex Basement
7, Meerabai Marg (Behind Jawahar Bhawan)
Lucknow 226 001 U.P. (INDIA)
Tel. : 91-522-2209542, 2209543, 2209544, 2209545
Fax : 0522-4045308
E-Mail : ibdco@airtelmail.in

First Edition 2010

Price: Rs. 99/-

ISBN 978-81-8189-486-1

Composed & Designed at :

Panacea Computers
2nd Floor, Agarwal Sabha Bhawan, Subhash Mohal
Sadar Cantt., Lucknow-226 002
Phone : 0522-2483312, 9335927082, 9452295008
E-mail : prasgupt@rediffmail.com

Printed at:

Salasar Imaging Systems
C-7/5, Lawrence Road Industrial Area
Delhi - 110 035
Tel. : 011-27185653, 9810064311

Message

I appreciate the efforts put in by my fellow-vets, Dr. Shridhar and Dr.Arun in bringing out a beautiful and handy book on pet dog care.

Dogs have become an integral part of our families and their well being is as important as that of our children. Pet-parents, especially the new ones face a lot of difficulties in raising their pets. Being in this line for more than two decades, the authors know their problems very well and hence have tried to describe in detail about various aspects of pet care in an easily understandable language. The measures suggested by authors in routine care of our pet-friends not only help in improving their health but also bring about a harmonious relationship with the pet-parents enriching their lives.

This book will surely help as a valuable guide to all dog-lovers and dog-breeders. I hope that the authors will come out with many more such useful books.

Hearty Congratulations.

Dr. S.Yathiraj,
M.V.Sc., Ph.D.,
Dean, Veterinary College,
Bangalore.

Our sincere thanks to

- All the pet lovers who encouraged us to write this book.
- Smt. Chitkala and Smt. Sreejaya for proof-reading the manuscript.
- Dr. B.C. Ramakrishna, Editor, Pet India, for providing beautiful photographs of various dog breeds.
- Dr. S. Yathiraj, Dean, Bangalore Veterinary college for his expert opinion about this book.
- Fellow vets for their whole-hearted support.
- India Book House, Lucknow, for excellent printing of this book.

Preface

Dog, man's Best Friend is the epitome of loyalty. It becomes an integral part of the family. Having a pet at home is fun, but at the same time, much demanding.

Lots of questions arise when one decides to welcome home a puppy. It is better to be prepared for various adjustments. Being in this field for more than two decades, we keep on facing many questions from the pet owners on a daily basis.

It was thought that it would be useful to all if we could bring out the answers to such questions in a book form. This book will be useful to a would-be pet owner, new pet owner, as well as to a seasoned pet owner. If this book would be able to answer your various questions about your pet, our aim will be fulfilled.

Dr N.B.Shridhar

Dr.C.S.Arun

A Dog's Plea

Treat me kindly, my beloved friend for no heart in all this world is more grateful for kindness than the loving heart of me

Do not break my spirit with a stick for though I should lick your hand between blows, your patience and understanding will more quickly teach me the things you would have me learn

Speak to me often, for your voice is the world's sweetest music, as you must know by the fierce wagging of my tail, when your footsteps fall upon my waiting ear

Please take me inside when it is cold and wet for I am a domesticated animal, no longer accustomed to bitter elements

I ask no greater glory than to have the privilege of sitting at your feet beside the hearth

Keep my pan filled with water for I can't tell you when I suffer thirst

Feed me clean food that I may stay well, to romp and play and do your bidding, to walk by your side, and stand ready, willing, and able to protect you with my life, should your life be in danger

And my friend, when I am old, and no longer enjoy good health and sight, do not make heroic efforts to keep me going, I am not having fun

Please see that my trusting life is taken gently

I shall leave this earth knowing with the last breath I draw that my fate was always safest in your hands

A pet parent's letter

I always dreamt of owning a dog during my childhood. I could not, because of various reasons. Now, being independent, I thought of bringing home a puppy. When I enquired in the market, I was bewildered by the array of breeds available. Also each one whom I contacted thought that he is an expert in the matters of dogs and gave me loads of advice. Finally, I decided to consult the real experts, i.e. the pet-vets. I had an opportunity to have a dialogue with Dr. Arun, a pet practitioner and Dr. Sridhar, an academician, both having more than two decades of experience in this field. I bombarded them with questions on all aspects of dog rearing to which they have given satisfactory answers. This question-answer session will definitely prove to be a valuable guide to any dog lover, be it a novice or an experienced one. If you have any further queries please feel free to contact these vets. They will definitely help you to have a harmonious relationship with your pet.

Contents

Chapter 1

Origin and Utility of Dogs

How did the dogs originate?

The origin of dogs is traced back to 40 million years. A creature called "Miacis", resembling wolves, is thought to be the ancestor of dogs.

Since how long the dogs are associated with human beings?

The co-existence of humans and dogs is evident from 10,000 BC onwards.

How useful are the dogs?

Dog is the most useful animal to human beings. In the yesteryears they were mostly utilized for hunting and guarding purposes and also in wars. As their other virtues were recognized, efforts were made to develop a breed to be utilized for a certain purpose. Dog's superior auditory and olfactory abilities make them a natural choice for crime investigations. They are useful in the rescue operations, be it in the snowy mountains, dense forests or turbulent rivers. Blind people find an excellent guide in dogs.

Our canine companions are playing an important role in medical research also. Many of them are sacrificing their lives, being experimental animals to develop treatment regimen for dangerous diseases like diabetes, pellagra, rickets, etc. Dog's never-ending love and affection is a sure-shot remedy for many types of mental disorders. Loneliness in this modern world can be alleviated easily through the no-strings-attached companionship provided by pooches. An adorable dog in the family helps the children to develop virtues like love, affection, caring, responsibility, etc. It helps the adults in the family to discipline their life-styles.

Are there any hitches associated with dogs?

Bringing a dog home is a responsibility which may last for at least a decade. A puppy will take away a lot of your leisure time. His naughty behaviour may test your patience. When some family members do not like the presence of a dog at home, it may evoke disputes. A barking or biting dog may irritate the neighbours which may lead to quarrels. An ill-cared dog may harbour diseases which are communicable to humans. So it is imperative on the part of a family to be well prepared before welcoming a pooch into its folds.

Stella and Bella, spitz dogs traveled in space in August 1960

Chapter **2**

Common Breeds of Dogs

How many dog breeds are there?

There are thousands of breeds of dogs of which more than 400 are recognized by FCI (Federation Cynologique Internationale).

How are dog breeds classified?

Dog breeds may be classified based on their utility. The different groups are,

a. Working dogs - German Shepherd, Boxer, Collie, Shetland Sheep Dog, Welsh Corgi, Borzoi, Doberman, Rottweiler, St. Bernard, etc.

b. Hunting dogs - Blood Hound, Afghan Hound, Basset Hound, Dachshund, Gray Hound, Saluki, Mudhol Hound, Labrador Retriever, Golden Retriever, Cocker Spaniel, Fox Terrier, Irish Setter, Beagle, Pointer, Weimeraner, etc.

c. Companion dogs - Pomeranian, Spitz, Lhasa Apso, Poodle, Pekingese, Pug, Papillon, Chihuahua, Chow Chow, Bull Dog, Dalmatian, Great Dane, Tibetan Terrier, etc.

Studies by German Economic and Social Community revealed that pet owners live a long and healthy life

Which is the most popular dog breed?

As per many surveys conducted, German Shepherd is the most popular breed. It is also known as Alsatian because of its origin from Alsace-Lorraine region of Germany. This breed is developed from a range of shepherding dogs in Germany by the efforts of GSD Club formed by Capt. Max Van Ṡtephaniz in 1899.

GSD is a strong, intelligent, obedient, courageous and faithful dog. It may be smooth-coated or bushy. The coat colors may be a mixture of black, grey, tan, brown, orange and yellow.

Height: 19-25 inches   Weight: 28 to 40 kgs

GSDs are mainly used as police dogs, guide dogs, and rescue dogs. They are excellent guard dogs since they are very loyal to their family. A German Shepherd dog needs regular exercise, grooming, and cleaning of ears.

How did the breed name Doberman originate?

A German tax collector by name Karl Freidrich Louis Doberman developed this breed, hence the name.

Dobermans are highly active, courageous, and intelligent dogs. With proper training they will be very good-watch dogs. Their hair coat is smooth and black, brown, blue or ash colored with tan markings. Tail is docked.

Height: 25-27 inches   Weight: 20-28 kgs

Proper exercise and handling are very important factors to be considered while bringing up a Doberman pup.

An old English Mastiff dog by name 'Zorba' weighed 155.58 kgs leading her into Guiness records

Which is the most sought after guard dog now-a-days?

More and more people like to have a Rottweiler as a guard dog now-a-days. It's a strong dog developed from the Molossus dog of Italy bred to fight lions in Roman amphitheatre. It traveled along with Roman army into Rottwil (Red Villa) village of Southern Germany where it became very popular. Hence the name Rottweiler.

Rotts are always black with rust markings. The tail is docked short. A well-bred Rottweiler is calm, confident and courageous with an aloofness towards strangers and a reserved attitude.

Height: 23-28 inches   Weight: 40-50 kgs

Ample exercise and training is a must for this breed.

Which is the dog breed well-known for its rescue operations?

It is the St. Bernard. This breed has its origin as a hospice dog in the Swiss Alps. It was originally used as a guard dog and to haul carts of milk. Their real worth as rescue dogs eclipsed these uses. Because of their thick coat and their outstanding sense of smell they have saved thousands of humans buried in the snow banks. It is a huge dog with short or long coat with a combination of tan and white color.

Height: 24-36 inches   Weight: 70-95 kgs

This breed needs a moderate amount of exercise and basic training.

'I see pet' service in Japan provides continuous contact between the pet and its owner through internet

Where did the breed Labrador Retriever come from?

Surprisingly, the breed Labrador Retriever did not come from Labrador island. He is actually from Newfoundland. Labradors are powerful, short-haired dogs used as agile land-and-water retrievers with extraordinary nose. They are very friendly with children. This solidly built dog may have hair coat colored black, yellow or chocolate color.

Labradors today are raised mainly as companion and guide dogs. They are very useful in crime detection also.

Height: 22-24 inches Weight: 27-34 kgs

Labradors should have proper exercise and controlled diet.

Why did this dog breed get the name 'Boxer'?

The breed got the name 'Boxer' because of its punchy fighting style. Though in olden times, Boxer was a ferocious dog, today it is a very loving family companion. Originated in Germany, it is mainly used for guarding, police and military work and in circuses. George Alt developed this breed.

Boxer's body is powerful and compact with a shiny coat colored fawn, brindle or shades of red with white markings. Always keen to work and play, Boxers need a lot of human company.

Height: 20-24 inches Weight: 25-32 kgs

Boxers need a dominant owner. They should be properly trained at an young age. They do well in temperate climates.

A dog flea can jump upto 350 times its bodylength! It is like a man jumping from one end to other of a football ground

Which is the fastest breed of canines?

Grey Hound is the fastest of all dog breeds. It can reach speeds of up to 72 kmph. Originated in Central Asia, Grey Hound is the oldest pure bred dog. Its origin dates back to over 4000 years. Grey Hounds were the most valuable possession of the Egyptian pharaohs. It is the only canine breed to be mentioned in the Bible.

It is a tall, elegant, deep-chested, smooth-coated dog with a lean but powerful body suited for running. Grey Hound comes in all colors, but not really grey. It is not hyperactive or aggressive, but is gentle and sensitive. It is extremely intelligent and loyal. It is very clean and does not have a doggy odor.

Grey Hound hunts by sight and not by smell. It is well known for its blood-donation capabilities.

Height: 26-30 inches   Weight: 24-36 kgs

Grey Hounds need enough exercise. Due to their design, they have difficulty in sitting and hence should not be forced to sit.

Which giant breed is the most popular one in India?

Among the giant breeds, Great Dane is the most popular one in our country. Though the name is 'Dane°, the origin of this breed is Germany. Known as the 'Apollo of all dogs', the Great Dane is a spirited, courageous and friendly dog.

The Dane has short and thick hair coat with a glossy appearance. Color may be black, blue, fawn, brindle or harlequin.

A Chihuahua dog in China protected and reared a poultry chick

Height: 28-42 inches   Weight: 45-55 kgs

Being a huge breed, this dog needs a lot of space and food. He should be trained properly in his early puppyhood. Caution should be exercised while small children play with this gentle giant.

Which is the breed associated with Buddhist spirituality?

Lhasa Apso, also called 'Lion Dog' or 'Prayer Dog' is often identified with Buddhism and The Dalai Lama. It went along with Buddhist monks from India to the other parts of the world. Tibetans believed that after the death of the owner his soul will enter into the Lhasa Apso dog. Considered as a lucky dog, it was solely owned by Monasteries and Emperors, and was given as gift to dignitaries. The Lahsas were used to guard the inner court of The Dalai Lama because of their acute hearing and quick reflexes. They are also known for their athletic nature.

Lhasa Apso is a furry dog and comes in black, white, brown, gold and combination of these colors.

Height: 10-11 inches   Weight: 6-7 kgs

Being a hairy breed, it needs daily grooming and proper care of the eyes and ears.

Are the Bull Dogs bred for bull fighting?

Before 1835, bull-fighting was a popular sport in the UK wherein the breed Bull Dog was used especially for this purpose. The Bull Dog's famous lock-jawed tenacity enabled him to clamp the opponent until he dropped. That is history. Today's bull-dog is a very mild-mannered dog. It is a

---

Eleven dogs involved in rescue operations during 9/11 disaster, died due to inhalation of toxic gasses and dust

courageous watch-dog.

Having a pear-shaped body and smooth coat, bull-dogs come in red, white, cream colors and in their combination.

Height: 16-18 inches   Weight: 20-25 kgs

Bull-dogs do not tolerate hot climates. They should be moderately exercised. Skin folds should be cleaned regularly.

Are Pomeranians also called German Spitz?

No. Though they look somewhat similar, they are entirely different dog breeds. Pomeranians are short, compact dogs, highly-active and buoyant dogs. Developed in Germany, they come in all colors and their mixtures. They have a soft, fluffy under coat and a long, harsh outer coat. Tail is high set, turned over the back and profusely covered with hair. Being highly intelligent, they learn tricks easily and hence are used more in circuses. They are very good indoor dogs.

Height: 9-11 inches   Weight: 1.5-3.5 kgs

They should be properly groomed to keep the coat healthy.

Spitz dogs also look like Pomeranians, but are of medium size. They come in all colors and are moderately coated.

Height: 10-18 inches   Weight: 8-15 kgs

Spitz dogs need obedience training in puppyhood.

Which is the 'Spotted' dog breed?

Dalmatian is the dog having black or brown spots on a clean white coat. It originated from Dalmatia, a part of West Yugoslavia, and hence the name. Being very versatile in

---

More than a million Americans have willed their property to their pets

utility, Dalmatian was used as a hunter, herder, ratter, companion or coach dog. He is also known as a 'fireman's friend' because of his use in saving lives in fire accidents.

Dalmatians are athletic, medium-sized and short-coated dogs. They are well known for long-distance endurance. At birth, the fur is pure white, and the spots appear by about 2 weeks of age. Coin-sized, black or brown spots develop fully within one year.

Height: 21-24 inches Weight: 22-25 kgs

Being energetic, Dalmatians need a lot of exercise. Also they should be checked for congenital deafness.

Which is the breed that appears in Vodafone TV ads?

It is the Pug dog which follows the boy wherever he goes. This ad increased the breed's popularity tremendously.

Pugs originated in China. They have been noted as early as 400 BC. Merchants made this breed popular in Europe. Pugs were named as national breed of Holland as one of them saved the life of Prince of Orange Province.

Pugs have small and steady body with a coat colored silver, apricot, or fawn.

Height: 10-11 inches Weight: 6-8 kgs

Pugs are well-suited for apartment living. Being short snouted, they do not tolerate hot weather.

Who developed Golden Retriever breed of dogs?

Lord Tweedmouth of Scotland developed the beautiful breed

Basenji dogs do not bark

of Golden Retriever through some dogs he bought from a circus company. They were mainly used to retrieve the game. Now-a-days, they are mainly used as companion dogs as they have very sweet temperament. They are also used for police work. These golden-colored dogs have long hair that needs proper attention.

Height: 20-24 inches Weight: 27-36 kgs

Goldies like swimming. They need proper exercising and grooming.

Where did the breed Dachshund originate?

Dachshunds originated in Egypt. They are bold, entertaining and friendly dogs. Dachshunds have a short but long body. Coat may be smooth or hairy. Color varies between a mix of black and tan or brown and tan, yellow or red.

Height: 8-11 inches Weight: 5-11 kgs

Dachshunds need enough exercise to avoid being obese.

Which breed of dogs was developed to hunt the bird 'Wood Rock'?

Cocker spaniel was developed to hunt Wood Rock and also other kind of birds. It is well-versed in tracking and retrieving also. Now-a-days it is raised more like a companion dog. In a recent survey, it was the second most popular breed in the USA.

Developed in Spain, this friendly dog is medium-built, having a hairy coat and long, pendulous, hairy ears. Coat color varies from black, red, brown, golden, orange, blue, or a

---

Icrisat company of Andhra Pradesh is developing an Anti-Rabies vaccine to be given through genetically modified groundnut

combination of these.

Height: 15-17 inches   Weight: 12-16 kgs

These dogs need daily grooming. Ears should be cleaned regularly. It is better to feed them in narrow and deep vessels to avoid the ears becoming wet.

Which local breed of Karnataka is recognized internationally?

Mudhol Hound of Karnataka is an internationally acclaimed breed. Its native place is Mudhol Town of Bagalkot district. Mainly developed for hunting, it has a long and slender body with sleek and strong legs. Coat is smooth and comes in all colors.

Height: 24-28 inches   Weight: 22-26 kgs

Being highly-active and spirited dogs, Mudhols need a lot of exercise.

To which breed do our country dogs belong?

Our country dogs do not conform to any particular breed specifications. Hence they are commonly known as Pie Dogs or Mongrels.

Mongrels come in all colors and their mixes. Coat may be smooth or short or long-haired. Body height and weight vary depending upon the parents and the nutrition they get. Generally, these dogs are sturdy, faithful, and make wonderful watch-dogs. They are very well-suited for farm conditions.

'Billi ' a Bull Terrier caught 400 mice in 17 hours. It has another record of catching 100 mice in 5 ½ minutes

Chapter **3**

Selection of a Dog

What are the factors to be considered before bringing a puppy home?

The main factors to be considered for the purpose of having a dog at home are the availability of space, your lifestyle, and capacity to spend on a dog. Availability of breed, veterinary care, acceptance by family members and neighbours are also to be considered.

Which breed is good?

It depends on the purpose for which you need a dog.

German Shepherds, Rottweilers, Dobermans make good watch-dogs. Mudhols and Mongrels suit well for farm conditions. Giant dog lovers may go for st. Bernard, Great Dane or Mastiffs. Ideal family dogs are Labrador, Golden Retriever, Spaniel, Beagle, etc. Pomeranian, Pug, Pekingese, Poodle, or Dachshund are good for apartment living.

Please refer Table 1 which highlights the various characters of different dog breeds.

Shall I bring a male or female?

Generally, males are more boisterous compared to females. They need more space, exercise and training. Females are

Bedudian nomads of Arabia have the family history of their Saluki dogs for more than 1000 years

mild and affectionate. They easily get adjusted with the family.

Are pure-bred dogs better or Mongrels?

It is a nice feeling to have a good-looking dog at home. But more the purity, more the puppy cost and its maintenance. Cross-bred or mongrels are relatively cheaper and easier to maintain. It is a noble thing to adopt a mongrel. The dog will always reciprocate with its loyalty and affection.

Where do I get a puppy from?

Always buy the puppy from reputed breeders or known persons. Insist on seeing both the parents or at least the mother. It will give you an idea of puppy's adult features. Even when brining a mongrel, better to get it from known sources.

How to select a puppy?

For this take the help of your Vet or an experienced friend. Puppies have to be selected based on the breed characteristics, health, growth, and activity.

Ideally, puppies in the age group of 1-2 months should be adopted.

What may be the cost of a puppy?

The cost of the puppy varies depending on the breed, its pedigree, sex and availability. Rarer the breed, higher the cost. Puppies of champion dogs may cost hundreds of thousand rupees. Approximate rates of some of the pups are like as under.

First year in the life of a dog is equal to 20 human years. Thereafter each dog year is equal to 7 human years

Spitz , Pomeranian Rs. 1,000 - 2,000/-

Dachshund, Lhasa Apso,

Doberman, Mudhol Rs. 2,000 - 3,000/-

German Shepherd, Labrador,

Golden Retriever, Irish Setter Rs. 3,000 - 5,000/-

Great Dane, Rottweiler,

Mastiffs Rs. 6,000 - 15,000/-

Pug, St. Bernard Rs. 15,000 - 30,000/

How much will it cost for the maintenance of the puppy?

You may have to shell out Rs. 500 – 3,000/ per month on maintenance of your puppy depending on the breed and feed.

TABLE 1

Breed	Size	Watch Dog	Friendly With Children	Exercise Needed	Grooming Needed
Boxer	**	**	***	***	*
Cocker Spaniel	*	*	**	**	***
Dachshund	*	***	**	**	
Dalmatian	***	**	**	***	*
Doberman	***	****	*	***	*
German Shepherd	***	****	**	***	**
Golden Retriever	***	**	***	***	***
Great Dane	****	**	***	***	*
Irish Setter	***	**	***	***	**
Labrador	***	*	***	***	**
Lhasa Apso	*	***	*	**	****
Pug	*	**	***	**	*
Rottweiler	***	****	*	***	*
Spitz	**	**	*	**	**
St. Bernard	****	*	**	***	**

Dogs are not allowed in public parks of Madhya Pradesh. Trespassers will be fined Rs.500/-

Chapter **4**

Care and Management of Puppy

What arrangements have to be made to welcome home a puppy?

- Choose a short and sweet name.
- Provide food and water bowls.
- Provide soft washable bedding.
- Provide toys that are large and sturdy.
- Choose the right collar and leash.
- Be prepared to give him constant company in the first few days.

What should I feed him initially?

Ideally, he should be fed what he was used to in the mother's house. Otherwise, he may be put on commercially available puppy foods. If they are not available, feed him with easily digestible semi-solid foods like rice, ragi or soji porridge. By 6 to 8 weeks of age, gradually introduce commercial puppy food, rice, chapatti, idli, dosa, boiled eggs, meat, fruits and raw or cooked vegetables.

Sarama, Shyama, Shabala are the names of dogs reared by Gods as mentioned in Rigveda

How much should I feed my puppy?

Please refer Table 2 for the approximate quantity and frequency of feeding. If you are feeding him a commercial food, follow the manufacturer's instructions.

TABLE 2

Quantity of semi-solid food to be fed to the dogs per day (in grams)

Age	Small breed	Medium breed	Large breed	Giant breed	Frequency of feeding
Up to 3 months	200 – 350	250 – 500	600 – 850	750 – 950	5 – 6 times
3 to 6 months	350 – 600	600 – 800	800 – 1200	1000-1500	3 – 4 times
6 – 12 months	600 – 800	800 – 1000	1200 –1600	1600-2200	2 – 3 times
After 12 months	800 – 1000	1000 - 1400	1600 –2000	2200-3000	2 times

Clean drinking water should always be available.

How to potty train my puppy?

The best way is to provide him frequent opportunities to go out and do it. After every meal, nap and a playtime take him out and allow him for a few minutes. Whenever he does it outside, praise him.

Please remember that an unvaccinated puppy should not be taken outside to the street. Let him relieve himself in your compound or on the terrace.

Never punish him for dirtying inside the house. With patience and praise, he will learn quickly.

Lyka is the first dog to travel to space on 3rd November 1957 by Sputnik-2

How to keep my puppy clean?

Dogs in general, and puppies in particular, do not need frequent bathing. Puppies may start having their regular baths only at or after 3 months of age. Until then, if they are dirty, give them a sponge bath and dry properly. To keep them clean, brush the coat daily with a suitable grooming brush. This will help in clearing-off the dirt, dust and dead hairs, improve blood circulation to skin and make it shiny.

Adult dogs may be bathed once in 2 to 4 weeks using a dog soap or shampoo.

Does my puppy need regular exercise?

Your puppy is a bundle of energy. He needs proper exercising, so that his energy is spent positively. He has to be engaged in playing with people or other dogs, long walks, obedience training and chewing. Otherwise, he may tend to develop destructive manners.

What is the deworming schedule for my puppy?

Your puppy has to be dewormed first at 3-4 weeks of age and then, once a month till 3 months of age to remove round worms, hook worms, and tape worms. Thereafter, it has to be repeated once in 3 months, or whenever worms are found in the stools.

Why should I get my puppy vaccinated?

Your puppy has to be vaccinated to protect him against fatal diseases like Canine Distemper, Parvo, Adeno, Corona, Parainfluenza viral infections, and Leptospirosis. Anti-rabies

---

Fido, a soldier's dog, unaware of his owner's death, used to wait daily for him in the bus stand for 17 years

vaccination is also a must to protect the puppy and also yourself against rabies. Please consult your veterinarian about the vaccination schedule.

Any other care necessary to keep him healthy?

Puppy's eyes should be cleaned with dry or wet cotton to remove adhering secretions. Ears should be cleaned with dry cotton once a week to remove the wax or debris. Never use ear buds.

Puppy's teeth should be brushed routinely with puppy brush and paste. His nails should be trimmed whenever needed. Your vet or groomer will help you in doing this.

Your puppy or dog may need additional supplements in the growing period. Provide them as per the vet's advice. Also you will have to take periodical ectoparasite control measures to make him free of fleas, ticks and lice.

Chitrasal lake and temple are built in honour of Chitra, the dog's loyalty

Chapter **5**

Training Your Puppy

Is training my puppy essential?

Training your puppy is nothing but inspiring confidence in him to enjoy a mutually beneficial relationship. It will establish you as the leader and the pet will enjoy the rewards you give him by way of praise, smile, loving touch, and a tasty treat.

Can I train my puppy myself?

Yes, you can train him yourself, provided, you are assertive with him since beginning. If not, you have to take the help of professional trainers.

What are the things needed for training?

The things you need are choke chain, 4-6 feet long leash, some treats, enough time, patience and a calm place.

What are the basic commands a puppy should learn?

A puppy should learn to 'sit', 'down', 'come', 'heel', 'stay', 'fetch' and 'don't touch' when you command him to do so.

How to train my puppy?

Start training the puppy by about 3 to 4 months of age. Take

Dogs have 6th sense. When cine actor William Cherry was murdered at London, pet Fox Terrier in his home at Beeford acted violently

him to a calm place and impart training for about 15 to 30 minutes daily. Give commands in a firm tone. Praise him a lot when he obeys. Reward him but never punish him.

To '**sit**' – Leash the puppy and have him on your left side. Hold the leash in your right hand, command 'SIT' and with the left hand, press his back near the base of the tail and simultaneously pull the leash. Once he learns this, teach him without using the leash.

To '**down**' - Let the puppy sit in front of you. Command 'DOWN' and slowly pull the front legs forward so that he will lie down. Later teach him to do this without pulling the legs.

To '**come**' – Leash the puppy and make him sit in front of you at a distance. Call his name, and command 'COME' with affection and simultaneously pull the leash slowly. Once he learns it, teach him without using the leash.

Never use this command to punish him.

To '**heel**' – Have the leashed puppy on your left side, command 'HEEL', start walking, and slowly pull the leash. If he goes forward, say 'NO', and pull the leash backwards. After he learns this, teach him to come with you without the leash.

To '**stay**' – Let the puppy stand in front of you. Point your fingers towards his eyes, command 'STAY' and move a few steps backwards. If he obeys, praise him. If he moves, firmly command 'NO, STAY'. Gradually increase the distance you move away from him. Command him to 'STAY' and

---

In Mahabharata, a dog follows Yudhistira during his final journey to heavens

disappear from his sight. When he obeys, reward him.

Teach him to follow this in sitting and lying positions also.

To **'fetch'** - Leash the puppy. Throw a ball or a wooden piece and loosen the leash. Praise him when he fetches it. If he is not interested in going, use a piece of bone or his toy. If he carries it in his mouth and doesn't want to give it to you, show him a treat and call affectionately. When he comes, take out the toy from his mouth and praise him. Do not use force. Gradually teach him to fetch without using the leash.

To **'don't touch'** - Let the leashed puppy stand besides you. Put the food in his bowl. When he wants to eat it, command 'DON'T TOUCH' and pull the leash backwards. When he stays quite, appreciate him. Once he learns this, try with different foods. Then, let other people give him food and make him learn not to touch it. Repeat the procedures without using the leash.

Obedience training will not happen overnight. Once taught with lots of patience, it will be a highly rewarding experience.

'Google' company workers may bring their pets to office. A study has shown that this practice has improved their work efficiency

Chapter 6

Breeding

Is breeding my dog essential?

No, breeding your dog is not very essential. Breed them only if you are sure of loving homes for them. Otherwise they will end up as strays. So get your dog neutered by about 6-12 months of age. This will prevent the incidence of mammary tumors, uterine infections, prostate diseases, etc.

When do the dogs mature?

Dogs usually mature by 6-12 months of age. Thereafter males will always be ready for intercourse. The females come to heat once in 5-6 months, during which there will be vaginal bleeding for 10-12 days. She will be receptive for the male towards the end of this period.

When should I get my dog bred?

Dogs in the age group of 1.5-6 years are best suited for breeding. Male dogs after one year of age and females in their second heat period can be used for breeding.

Bitches should be taken to the male dog in the end of the bleeding period i.e., 10-12 days in most of the cases. Best period for mating can be ascertained by doing laboratory tests. Mating should be arranged on alternate days till the

---

Mischelle, Trainer of Kaukapakapa, New Zealand was saved by her two pet dogs when she fell into a valley 150 feet deep

bitch refuses the male.

Do all mated dogs become pregnant?

Not necessarily. In many cases a bitch may not become pregnant due to various reasons.

How to confirm pregnancy?

Pregnancy in bitches can be confirmed by abdominal palpation by about 28 days post coitus. If scanning facilities are available, it can be done as early as 18 days. Radiographic confirmation is possible by about 42 days.

What is the pregnancy period in bitches?

Duration of pregnancy in bitches varies from 58 to 70 days.

What are the changes observed in a bitch during pregnancy?

In the first month, there will not be much physical change in a pregnant bitch. In the second month, gradually the abdomen starts distending, mammary glands develop and nipples become larger. By eight weeks, milk production may also start.

Behavioral changes may also be observed in pregnant bitches. They will become calm and less active and seek more affection from the owner. Some dogs may not eat much while some may eat voraciously.

Does any special care need to be taken during pregnancy?

A pregnant bitch has to be fed a balanced diet. If she cannot eat at one stretch, she has to be fed more often in divided

---

Cameroon Rab has invented a mobile phone especially for dogs involved in rescue operations

doses. Care should be taken to avoid obesity. She has to be given moderate exercise. As the date of delivery approaches, she has to be shifted to whelping kennel or a place where you want her to deliver the puppies.

What are the signs of delivery in bitches?

Generally, the bitch nearing parturition goes-off food. She may become excited or seek seclusion. She will start pawing and digging holes in the ground. The mammary glands get filled with milk. As the delivery time approaches, she starts panting. There will be a greenish black discharge from the vagina. Then she will start straining to push the puppy out.

How much time it will take to deliver all the puppies?

Generally delivery will be completed within 8-12 hours. It may even take up to 24 hours between the arrival of first and last puppy. Between two successive puppies the time gap may be from few minutes to few hours.

How to assist my dog during delivery?

Most of the deliveries happen without complications. If the bitch is straining for a long time without expulsion of puppy you have to call the Veterinarian. If the puppy is born with the umbilical cord intact, you may have to cut it using clean blade or scissors. After the delivery is completed please see that the mother and the puppies are together and comfortable. Puppies should drink mother's milk as early as possible. If the mother wants to eat or drink, you may give her the usual food or warm milk or little bit of glucose powder often.

Barbara Bush's book about 'Mili', her pet dog is a best seller

How to take care of newborn puppies?

For the first two weeks, mother will take care of the puppies. You should keep on watching the mother and the neonates to ascertain that they are together, are warm and each puppy is fed and cleaned by the mother. See that the umbilicus is properly dried and if needed apply some antiseptics. Frequently change the bedding to keep it dry.

If the mother lacks mothering instincts, she may not take care of her puppies. Then you should forcibly make her to feed the puppies. Make sure that all the puppies are fed properly. If she does not lick them, clean their bellies often with a cloth soaked in warm water simulating the mother's lick to stimulate bowel movements in puppies. If the mother's milk is not enough, take the help of a foster mother or feed them commercially available milk replacement or weaning food.

When will the puppy become independent of mother?

Newborn puppies crawl by one week and walk by three weeks of age. They open their eyes by 10-15 days. Milk teeth start appearing by three weeks of age. At this stage, if the mother is not interested in feeding the puppies, you may wean them and start giving them easily digestible puppy foods. By one month of age, they can be completely independent of mother.

During Tsunami, pet dog Selvakumar saved Dinakaran of Cudallore by pushing him onto a hillock

Chapter **7**

Common Diseases of Dogs and their Prevention

What are the causes of diseases in dogs?

Diseases in dogs are generally due to infection by viruses, bacteria, fungi or parasites. They may also occur due to deficiency or excess of nutrients, hormonal imbalance, allergy, accidents etc.

How to recognize that my dog is not well?

A diseased dog will not be active. He will not be interested in food. He may lose weight. There may be many other signs like excessive secretions from eyes, nose, ears or vagina, vomiting, diarrhoea, nervous signs, anaemia, skin rashes, pain, change in gait or posture, cough etc. depending on the system affected.

What to do when I notice these signs?

Immediately seek the advice of a veterinarian. Tell him in detail whatever you have observed. Follow his instructions meticulously.

How to prevent the occurrence of diseases in my pet?

Preventive measures start from the selection of a puppy. Always ensure that the puppy's parents are healthy and well cared for. Provide the puppy a clean and hygienic environment, balanced food and water, optimal exercise, grooming and other cares needed. Get him dewormed and vaccinated regularly as per the Vet's advice. Do not let him mix with unclean and unhealthy dogs. Do not take an unvaccinated puppy out on streets for walks. Get him treated immediately whenever he is not well. These steps will go a long way in disease prevention.

Which are the common Viral diseases that may affect dogs?

Common viral diseases that may affect dogs are as follows:

A. Canine Distemper - Caused by a Paramyxo virus, it is a highly infectious disease affecting all age groups. It spreads through the secretions of an infected animal and also through air. Main symptoms observed are high fever, anorexia, conjunctivitis, difficulty in breathing, vomiting and loose motions. Later on nervous signs like uncoordinated gait, lameness, paralysis or twitching of muscles in the legs, jaws or forehead are seen. Pregnant bitches may abort.

There is no specific treatment for this disease. Isolate the affected dog from others and get him palliative treatment.

Canine Distemper can be effectively prevented through timely vaccinations.

B. Canine Adeno Viral Infection - Canine Adenovirus Type

A Mongolian dog which has acted in the movie "Cave of Yellow Dog" was honoured in Cannes film festival

1 causes Infectious Canine Hepatitis, a fatal disease of dogs. It also affects the respiratory system leading to associated signs. All age groups are affected. The virus is secreted in urine, feces and saliva of affected dogs and spreads through contaminated food, cloth or utensils. Recovered dogs may also act as carriers.

Symptoms observed are high fever, vomiting, loose motion, inappetance, conjunctivitis, loss of voice, anemia, jaundice, bleeding through nose and urinary bladder, ascites(water belly) etc. In some dogs, eyes may become bluish or whitish leading to blindness in some cases. Puppies show high mortality rate.

Though there is no specific treatment for this disease, timely administration of fluids, antibiotics, hemotonics, liver tonics will help to reduce the severity of the disease.

Periodic vaccination and hygienic measures help in preventing this disease.

C. Parvo Viral Infection - This is one of the most dreaded viral infection of puppies. It is caused by Canine Parvovirus 2-A & 2-B of which the latter is highly pathogenic. Though it affects all age groups, the disease is severe in young puppies.

The disease is transmitted through ingestion of virus contaminated feces by pups. In the host body the virus gets localized in bone marrow and intestines and damages them leading to severe vomiting, bloody diarrhoea, anemia, dehydration and death. Survival rate is only 50-60% even with prompt and timely treatment. If the puppy survives first 4-5 days of infection, chances of recovery are high.

'Cho' a multipurpose dog of China has bluish-black tongue and almost straight hind legs

There is no specific treatment for this disease. Supportive care includes fluid therapy, antibiotics, electrolytes, blood transfusion etc.

To prevent the occurrence of this disease,

- keep your puppy isolated till its immunization schedule is completed,
- thoroughly clean the kennel, bedding and utensils with bleach solution,
- breeders should always get the bitch immunized prior to mating with live parvo virus and during pregnancy with killed parvo virus vaccine.

D. Corona Viral Infection - Caused by Canine Corona virus, symptoms of this disease are similar to that of Canine Parvo viral infection. Sometimes when both the viruses infect the puppy simultaneously, damage will be very severe leading death in most of the cases.

This infection can be effectively prevented through vaccinations.

E. Parainfluenza Viral Infection - Infection by parainfluenza virus leads to respiratory symptoms mainly dry cough. It is easily transmitted from one dog to another through air. It can be treated symptomatically with antibiotics, antihistamines and antitussives.

This infection can be prevented through vaccinations.

F. Rabies - This is the most dreaded and most discussed disease of dogs as it is communicable to human beings and is

---

In San Francisco, pet parents must provide good food and shelter to their pets as per an ordinance

always fatal. It affects all warm-blooded mammals, more often the wolves, jackals, dogs, cats, rats and bats.

Caused by a bullet-shaped virus called Rhabdovirus, this disease is usually transmitted through the saliva of an infected animal. The virus may remain dormant for a few weeks or years inside the body of the animal. It travels through nerves to the brain, multiply there and then get localized in the salivary glands. It gets transmitted to another animal through bite or contamination of wounds.

Rabies gets expressed either in Furious form or Dumb form.

In Furious form of Rabies, symptoms observed are excitement, continuous barking, excessive salivation, phobia towards light and water etc. Once these signs start, death is inevitable within a week's time.

In Dumb form of Rabies, affected dog will be dull and listless, seek seclusion, will be off-feed and may not bark. It is usually difficult to suspect Rabies in such cases.

Diagnosis is based on symptoms, biological tests and post-mortem examination of brain for Negri bodies.

There is no treatment for this disease. For prevention,

- do not neglect any animal bite,
- wash the bite wound thoroughly with water, soap and antiseptic solution,
- do not bandage or suture the wound as far as possible,
- take prompt medical advice to get Anti-Rabies vaccination.

Sonia Wild of UK had her Collie dog Lucy as her best woman during wedding ceremony

Since most of the times, Rabies occurs due to dog bites, get your pet dogs properly vaccinated as per the Veterinarian's advice.

Here are some more questions answered about Rabies-

- **How serious is Rabies viral infection?**

Rabies viral infection is always fatal. In our country every year more than 30,000 deaths due to this disease are recorded. Actual figures may be even higher because many cases go unreported.

- **Do all bites lead to Rabies?**

Not all bites by rabid animal will cause Rabies. Depending on the site of bite, virus load in the saliva, depth of the wound and number of people bitten by the same animal, the disease may or may not get transmitted. In infected cases, the symptoms of the disease may start appearing within a week or after few years also. So no bite should be neglected.

- **My pet is vaccinated. If he bites me, should I take Anti-Rabies Vaccine?**

Since the immune status of your pet cannot be ascertained always through laboratory tests, it is better to get the vaccine done as per the medical advice.

- **My pet is always indoors. Is it necessary to get him vaccinated?**

He has to be vaccinated because there is always a chance of he contracting the disease through rats, cats or some stray dog bite which may go unnoticed by you.

A dog owner of Seattle was fined 50000 dollars because his dog killed the neighbor's cat

- **My pet is vaccinated. If he is bitten by a stray dog, what should I do?**

Better to get him vaccinated as per the post-bite schedule. If the dog who has bitten your pet is healthy for 10 days, three doses of vaccine given on 0,3,7 days post-bite will be enough. If that dog dies within 10 days, then three more doses of vaccine on days 14, 28 and 60 post-bite should also be taken.

- **I don't know when my pet is vaccinated. What do I do?**

Get him vaccinated right now and after 3 weeks again if needed and thereafter once a year.

- **Should I get my pet Anti-Rabies vaccine before going abroad?**

Some countries have been declared as 'Rabies-Free'. When you go to such countries, your pet has to be given ARV and subsequently tested in lab for proper immune status. Details about these procedures may be had from the immigration authorities.

- **Is Rabies a communicable disease?**

No, it is not. But it may get transmitted through organ transplantation if the donor is rabid.

- **Are there different ARV s for different species of animals?**

No, the same ARV is used in all species of animals.

- **Can human ARV be used to protect my pet?**

You can get your pet cloned! Genetic Savings & Clone Inc of USA offers this service for 50000 dollars

Yes. It will be quite expensive.

- **Any adverse reaction to ARV?**

Not with the present day Tissue culture vaccines. Rarely some animals may develop fever after the vaccination.

- **If it is confirmed that my pet has Rabies, what should I do?**

Immediately isolate him. If possible get him euthanized. Get the ARV done for all the family members as per medical advice.

Which are the common Bacterial diseases of dogs?

Common Bacterial diseases of dogs are:

A. Leptospirosis- It is the most important bacterial disease of dogs as it is of zoonotic importance. More than 200 serovarieties of Leptospira may infect the dogs, but most common ones are L. canicola, L. icterohemmorhagiae, L. pomona and L. grippotyphosa. Incidence of the disease is more in male dogs. It is transmitted from one dog to another through the urine of affected dog. Rats also play a role in the transmission of Leptospirosis.

Main symptoms observed are dullness, inanition, vomiting, bleeding through nose or in urine, jaundice etc.

Early diagnosis and treatment with proper antibiotics and supportive therapy will help in curing this disease.

Effective vaccines are available to prevent this disease. Rat control measures should be undertaken in the kennels to aid

---

Dogs get worshipped at Nepal during Diwali

in preventing Leptospirosis.

B. Other Bacterial Diseases-Various types of bacteria like Streptococci, Staphylococci, E.coli etc may infect the dogs and cause many ailments. With timely antibiotic treatment, they can be cured effectively.

For prevention, hygienic practices have to be followed.

Which is the common Fungal disease of dogs?

The most common fungal disease of dogs is Ringworm. It is a skin infection caused by Trichophytan and Microsporum genera of fungi. Main symptoms of this disease is occurrence of circular patches of alopecia on skin associated with severe itching.

Ringworm can be diagnosed by using Wood's lamp. For treatment, antifungal shampoos, lotions, ointments and/or tablets have to be used, generally for a long time.

Hygienic measures have to be undertaken to prevent this disease.

Which Parasitic diseases affect dogs commonly?

External parasites like lice, ticks, fleas or mites and Internal parasites like roundworms, tapeworms, hookworms or spirocerca affect dogs commonly.

How to control ectoparasitic infestation of dogs?

Ectoparasites are mainly seen on the hairy areas of skin, inside the ears and in between the toes. Some of them complete their life-cycle on the dog's body and some in the

---

Bangalore PFA has started a burial ground for pets

environment. They may be present in the surroundings of kennel, on the floor, clothing, grass, plants, crevices of doors or windows etc.

Ectoparasitic infestation leads to severe pruritus, anemia and dermatitis. They also act as intermediate hosts for tapeworms.

Ectoparasites can be eliminated from dog's body using suitable medicated soap or shampoos, powders or collars. Oral tablets, injections or drop medicines are also available to get rid of them. For effective control, the environment around the dog should also be made free of ectoparasites by periodical spraying of suitable insecticide.

How serious is endoparasitic infestation of dogs?

Endoparasites live inside the dog's body, mainly in intestines, lungs, liver, oesophagus, heart or eyes. They get transmitted through ingestion of contaminated food and water or through ectoparasites. Transmission from mother to puppies may occur inside the womb or through mother's milk. Inside the host's body, they utilize all the nutrients available making him weak and debilitated with stunted growth. Other signs like vomiting, bloody diarrhoea, cough, itching, sudden death etc., may also be observed. Worms or their segments will be seen in the feces or in the vomitus.

Type of worm infecting can be diagnosed by doing the fecal examination and treated specifically. But in practice, broad spectrum anti-parasitic medicines are given in combination to eliminate all types of worms.

For control, dogs have to be dewormed regularly. Hygienic

Gunthur IV, a German Shepherd is the richest dog on earth. He is worth 180 million pounds. He inherited this from his father Gunthur III

practices are to be followed.

Any other important disease that may trouble dogs?

Many other diseases are commonly seen in dogs, owing to a variety of causative factors. Most important of them are,

A. Rickets - It is a disease of puppies caused due to deficiency or malabsorption of Calcium, Phosphorus or Vitamin D. This leads to weakness of bones manifested by bow legs. Affected puppy finds it difficult to walk.

Rickets has to be diagnosed early and treated promptly. Otherwise deformity will be life-long.

For prevention, always feed a balanced food to the puppy. Let him get exposed to early morning sunlight.

B. Seizures - Seizures or fits may be seen in dogs of all ages. Though exact reason is not known, various factors are thought to be associated with it, e.g., difficulty during puppy's birth, head injuries, worm infestations, toxins, heart or kidney diseases, tumors, diseases of central nervous system, low glucose levels, deficiency of Calcium, B complex vitamins, etc.

Onset of seizures is usually sudden and unexpected. Dog may salivate a lot, may stay immobile or run around aimlessly. It may become unconscious, kick the limbs involuntarily, may urinate and defecate. In partial seizures, there may be head turning, licking, jaw snapping, movement of a single limb or behavioral changes.

Immediate steps to treat the disease are to see that the dog is

---

A popular TV actor dog Eddi, earns 6000 pounds per episode

not disturbed, placed in a warm, dimly lit room without any sharp object nearby. The fits episode may last for a few minutes. Consult the Vet to start medication if needed. Seizures may get controlled with a few weeks of medication. But in some dogs, life-long treatment may be needed. In such cases, goal of treatment will be to control the seizures with minimal adverse effect of drugs.

C. Pyometra - It is a condition wherein there is accumulation of pus in the uterus. It is commonly seen in old bitches, especially the ones who have not whelped. Affected dog gradually becomes dull and off-feed. It may drink lot of water and vomit. In open type of pyometra, there will be foul smelling, bloody or purulent discharge from the vagina.

This disease can be diagnosed through blood tests, scanning or radiography. Mild cases may respond to antibiotic therapy. Surgical removal of uterus has proven to be beneficial.

For prevention, always get the bitches spayed at an early age.

How to nurse the ill dogs?

Compassionate nursing helps the dogs to recover fast from a disease. Please follow these guidelines –

- Separate the diseased dog and place him in a calm and warm place.
- Administer the medications as per the Vet's advice.
- Feed easily digestible food in divided quantities.

- If he is not taking food, feed glucose or tender coconut water or honey.
- Lift and take him out often to help him evacuate the bowels and bladder.
- Change the bedding if it is wet.
- If it is a communicable disease, be careful about personal hygiene.

Do we get any disease from dogs?

Yes, some diseases like Rabies, Leptospirosis, Brucellosis, Giardiasis, Ringworm, Scabies are communicable to humans. Also, intermediate stages in the life-cycle of some parasites may infect the human beings.

How to avoid contracting diseases from dogs?

Take utmost care about personal hygiene. Clean the dog house and surroundings regularly. Do not feed raw meat or fish to the dog. Deworm and vaccinate him periodically. Separate the infected dog from other dogs and children.

'Dr. Dog' project of Animal Asia Foundation offers soothing company of a lovely dog to bring people out of depressions

Chapter 8

First-Aid in Dogs

Which are the common conditions that need First-Aid?

Emergencies like haemorrhages, fractures, choking, toxicity and snake bites need treatment in dogs.

How to arrest bleeding from wounds?

Whenever there is bleeding, press and hold for a few minutes, a cotton ball soaked in an antiseptic lotion over the point of haemorrhage. If still not controlled place thick cotton balls over the wound and tie with a clean cloth or bandage. If the bleeding is in the tip of the tail or limbs, place a tight knot 1-2 inches above the bleeding point for a few minutes. If you suspect internal bleeding, check the conjunctiva for pallor. Do not disturb the dog as far as possible. Immediately seek veterinary help.

What to do if the dog's bones are broken?

Fracture of bones lead to swelling and severe pain in the affected part. The dog will limp as it cannot bear weight. It is imperative to see that proper immobilization of the fractured part is achieved; place strong wooden sticks, thin wooden sheets or thick pads of cloth around the fractured site and tie with a thread or cloth. Contact the vet immediately.

'Kandya', hunting dog owned by Chathrapathi Sahu Maharaj once saved him from a tiger. When the King died, Kandya also gave up his life

How to manage choking in dogs?

Dogs may try to eat many items available in their surroundings like balls, cloth, wire, plastic covers etc. Sometimes it may get stuck in the throat leading to choking. It has to be relieved immediately. Otherwise the dog may die due to asphyxia.

Try to open the dog's mouth widely holding with a cloth and remove the choking object using fingers or forceps. If it is a small object, feed bananas or bread soaked in milk so as to facilitate its movement into the stomach and out through the feces.

What to do in case of suspected poisoning?

Dogs may accidentally ingest many toxic things. In such cases, immediately induce vomiting by feeding little quantity of salt powder or saturated salt solution or 1% copper sulfate solution or mustard solution. If the dog is eating, feed him chilled raw egg white. If you know what poison the dog has ingested, give the details to the Vet so that he can give specific treatment.

What measures have to be taken in case of snake bite?

Snake bites are common with dogs living in farms. Dogs while trying to fight with snakes get bitten more on face and legs. If you can locate the point of bite, make a small incision there with a clean blade and let the blood flow out for a few minutes. If the bite is limbs or tail, put a know above the bite point and immediately seek Veterinary assistance. It is better to keep some stock of Anti-Snake venom in the farm.

A German Shepherd dog detected opium worth 3.5 million dollars hidden in a lorry load of onions

Chapter 9

Vices in Dogs and their Management

Which are the common bad habits that some dogs may develop?

Some dogs may develop bad habits like excessive barking, climbing over people, urinating everywhere, eating rubbish or fecal matter, stealing food, destroying house-hold articles or plants, chasing vehicles etc. This will cause disturbance to owners, neighbors, guests or other common people. Hence proper steps have to be taken to prevent these vices.

How to prevent my dog from developing bad habits?

Training in this regard should start from the puppy hood. All people who come in contact with the puppy should understand that their behavior will influence the puppy a lot and hence provide him a proper environment. When the puppy behaves in an undesirable way, show your displeasure sternly. Scold or punish him while he is misbehaving and not later. Praise and reward him when he behaves properly.

My dog barks a lot. What to do?

Dogs bark instinctively on seeing strangers or on hearing other dogs' voice. Apart from this, they bark a lot to protest against solitude. Try to avoid this situation. Spend more time with him. When he has to be left alone give him some toys or chews. You may also record your voice and play it on a tape recorder. Alternatively, switch on the radio in a low voice.

When he barks a lot in your presence, command "Quiet" and teach him to follow that.

How to avoid my dog jumping on people?

Dogs jump on people to show their love and affection. This behavior will be more pronounced when they see the master after a time gap. So do not make your home-coming a grand event. Do not immediately go to your dog and pet him. Whenever you attend to him, always discourage your dog jumping on you. Show your displeasure by sternly telling "No" and push him back. If needed hit him mildly with a paper roll.

How to prevent indiscriminate urination?

Weak and feeble-minded dogs urinate indiscriminately. Such behavior may also be observed when two or more dogs are there in a house. Each one urinates anywhere to show its dominance or opposition.

To prevent this, take your dog frequently out to encourage micturition. Support and encourage shy natured dogs to develop confidence. Do not punish them severely. Have lots of patience and teach them what to do.

Many a times this sort of behavior gets corrected automatically once the puppy matures physically and

---

About 250000 dogs were used in 2nd World War for various purposes

mentally.

My dog eats rubbish and fecal matter. How to avoid this?

Dogs become coprophagic when they have deficiency of nutrients, out of boredom, when they are chained for long time, due to lack of exercise or to attract attention. Consult your Vet to formulate a proper diet for your dog. Deworm if necessary. Engage him in activities. Provide him toys or chews to avoid boredom. After every meal take him for short walks and encourage defecating outside. Clean the surroundings immediately if he does it inside. You may try putting some neem oil over the fecal matter to distract him from eating it. If you observe him eating feces, sternly say "No" and reprimand him.

How to avoid my puppy chewing on things?

Puppies in their 'teething period', i.e., 2-6 months of age, tend to bite and chew whatever thing they get in their vicinity. Try to keep valuable and delicate things away from the puppy. If he is biting legs of chair or table, apply neem oil to them. Engage the puppy in some activity. Get him suitable toy or chews.

My dog chases moving vehicles. How to stop this?

Some dogs get excited and chase running vehicles. To avoid this, ride on your cycle or bike in front of him. If he starts chasing it, stop the vehicle, turn, face him and say 'No'. On repeatedly doing this, he will loose interest in chasing. If he still continues it, try to throw some water on his face through a sprayer, which will distract him from chasing the vehicles.

According to Egyptian mythology, a dog by name Arubis protects the graves

Chapter 10

Dog Shows

What is the aim of dog shows?

Each dog breed has got certain standards. Aim of dog shows is to compare and determine how far a particular dog has those qualities. It is a matter of pleasure and pride to raise a dog conforming to the highest standards. Also, that dog and its progeny will fetch a very good price. Hence many breeders will be interested in exhibiting their dogs in shows.

When did the dog shows begin?

First ever dog show was held in 1859 at Newcastle, U.K. In our country dog shows started in 1900 and are now being held regularly in all major cities. Small towns are not lagging behind and are also arranging dog shows.

Are there different types of dog shows?

Yes. Some shows are only for the dogs registered with the Kennel Clubs. Some are open to all. Also some dog shows will be conducted for a particular breed only.

How to take part in a dog show?

Preparation for a dog show starts with the selection of the puppy. A pup from a good line, preferably having some champion dogs, should be selected. He should be raised as per the breeder's recommendation and vet's advice with proper feeding and exercise. Obedience training is very essential. At a proper age, he should be exposed to the company of other dogs and crowd so that he will learn to behave properly in the ring.

Your dog has to be exhibited in the show in a particular category. Get the details from the organizers well in advance, fill up the entry form correctly and send along with the prescribed entry fees.

Before taking him to the show, please see that his deworming and vaccinations are completed. Wash him, dry with a soft cloth and groom him. Brush the coat of rough haired dogs nicely. Trim the nails, clean the teeth and eyes.

In the ring, exhibit him so that his virtues are clearly visible. This can be achieved with proper experience. You can also take the help of professional exhibitor for this purpose.

What happens in dog shows?

In a show, dogs of one particular breed will be examined at a time for their body conformation, standing, gait, condition of coat, teeth and eyes etc. Based on these, best male and female of that breed will be selected.

In the next stage, these selected dogs of different breeds will be examined in the ring and then the best dog of the show will be selected. Depending on the points they get, one to five places will be announced.

Aquadog, a cola drink for dogs is available in beef, chicken and bacon flavours

Chapter **11**

Miscellaneous Questions

How can I help my Vet in treating my dog?

Most of the Vets are busy as they will be providing mobile services most of the times. So a little help from your side will go a long way in solving your pet's problems. Here are a few suggestions in this regard-

- Get your dog obedience trained.
- Keep all his records at a handy place.
- Observe all the symptoms and report to the Vet.
- Be ready with the pet leashed and confined at the time of Vet's visit.
- Please remember that it is your responsibility to control your dog for examinations. Dog being apprehensive of Vet may not co-operate with him.
- Follow the Vet's instructions properly.

What is the vaccination schedule for my pet dog?

General vaccination schedule for your pet is as follows-

- 6th week - DHLPPiC primary vaccine
- 8th week - Anti-Rabies primary vaccine

Aristotle believed that Tibetan Mastiff dog is the result of breeding tiger with dog

- 9th week - DHLPPiC booster vaccine
- 11th week - Anti-Rabies booster vaccine

Thereafter every year DHLPPiC and Anti-Rabies vaccine have to be repeated.

Always consult your Vet to formulate a vaccination schedule for your pet depending on the local conditions.

What are the precautions to be taken before vaccination?

- Only healthy pets have to be vaccinated.
- Better to deworm the pet before vaccination.
- Cold-chain of the vaccine has to be maintained.
- Vaccine has to be injected aseptically.

Is neutering my pet essential?

Yes, if you are not interested in dog breeding, better to get your pet sterilized.

What are the advantages of neutering?

Neutering is a humane method of reducing the number of unwanted animals. It is a safe and effective surgery. In males, it prevents the chances of testicular tumors and prostate cancer. In females, it avoids the occurrence of pyometra, venereal diseases and mammary tumor.

Which is the best age for neutering?

Dogs and bitches can safely be sterilized by about six months of age. Bitches have to be sterilized before their first heat

---

Auditory capacity of dogs is five times that of human beings

cycle. This will greatly reduce the chances of breast cancer.

Where can I get good quality pups?

Following is a list of some kennels and breeders where you can get good quality pups-

1. ShepMagic kennels, Bangalore - 9845401111
2. Paradise kennels, Bangalore - 9986011576
3. Bluecross Vet polyclinic, Bangalore - 9341216168
4. Vinmin kennels, Chennai - 04424993481
5. Kalaivani kennels, Chennai - 09840359248
6. Van Jagsburg kennels, Bangalore - 08025540962
7. Yashbans kennels, Bangalore - 9844058080
8. Pragathi kennels, Bangalore - 9448544822
9. Anis kennels, Bangalore - 9901626262
10. Fan kennels, Coimbatore - 09843023567
11. Rajkamal kennels, Mysore - 9448342642
12. Laxmi Aquarium, Mysore - 9448787168
13. Mr.Mohan, Mysore - 9886208122

Where can I get food and accessories for my dog?

Here is a list of shops selling dog food and accessories-

1. The Pet Shop, Mehrauli, New Delhi 01132984950
2. Pet Land, New Delhi 01141551486
3. Mahesh Pet Point, New Delhi 9810098572

Bang, a Grey hound jumped 30 feet to get into Guiness book of world records

4. KPS, My Pet Shop, Mumbai 65914444
5. Universal Pet Store, Bangalore 9845459134
6. Kennel India, Bangalore 9845079234
7. Sarvodaya Agencies, Udipi 9448133325
8. Bright Shop, Bangalore 08025592475
9. Glenands, Bangalore 08025586932
10. Harshitha Enterprises, Bangalore 9845391191
11. C & T Pharma's Pet Shoppee, Bangalore 08023230237
12. SRK Pharma, Bangalore 08025532636
13. Preethi Vet Pharma, Mysore 08212421313
14. Laxmi Aquarium, Mysore 9448787168
15. Pet Fancies, Mysore 9449406770
16. Pet Care Clinic, Polibetta, Coorg 08274251313

Where can I leave my pet for boarding for a few days?

Here is a list of boarding kennels-

- Whispering kennels, Bangalore 9844004905
- Karuna, Bangalore 08023411181
- Sri Sai kennels, Bangalore 9886025572
- Pragathi kennels, Bangalore 9448544822
- Rajkamal kennels, Mysore 9448342642
- Laxmi Aquariums, Mysore 9448787168

Bhavanidut Joshi of Uttaranchal has willed his property to his pet dogs Shivraj and Tikaram

SOME INTERESTING FACTS ABOUT DOGS

* Shangret Dansas, a Great Dane measures 41.5″ tall
* A German Shepherd dog detected opium worth 3.5 million dollars hidden in a lorry load of onions
* Ella Vandal of NewYork has willed her property worth 15 million pounds to Toby, a poodle dog
* Smallest dog recorded is a Yorkshire Terrier which was 2.5″ tall and 3.75″ long. It weighed 113 grams only
* About 250000 dogs were used in 2nd World War for various purposes
* Adult dogs have 42 teeth
* Strongheart and Rintintin are famous movie star dogs
* First dog to act as blindmen's eye was a German Shepherd by name Buddy
* Timmy, a Grey hound has sired more than 3000 pups
* Grey hounds can run at a speed of 70 kms per hour
* Bluey, an Australian dog lived more than 29 years
* Bobby, a collie dog got lost in Indiana of USA. It took him six months to reach his hometown at Oregon 3000 miles away
* Columbus used cruel dogs to threaten the natives of newly found islands
* Hitler killed his dog Blondy so that it will not be adopted by non-Aryans

---

Bhola Munda of Ranchi was saved from a wild elephant attack by fierce barking of his pet dog

* Smoky, a Yorkshire Terrier helped Telecom people to lay the cables inside a pipe 70 feet long and 8 inches diameter
* Smuggling of dogs from Assam to Nagaland is very rampant
* Dogs when happy move their tail more to the right and when sad or angry move it more to the left according to a research conducted by Tristy University
* Special types of icecreams are available exclusively for dogs in Australia
* Bhavanidut Joshi of Uttaranchal has willed his property to his pet dogs Shivraj and Tikaram
* Fashion shows are conducted now-a-days to launch pet dresses
* Trained dogs can detect fake CDs by smell
* Many major metros of the world have 5 star hotels for dogs
* Aquadog, a cola drink for dogs is available in beef, chicken and bacon flavours
* Tillmok Cheddar, a Jack Russel Terrier has done hundreds of paintings which are sold for hundreds of dollars
* Chacolate, an Argentine dog protected a boy from bee stings but died in the process
* Bang, a Grey hound jumped 30 feet to get into Guiness book of world records

---

Bluey, an Australian dog lived more than 29 years

* Savar, a Doberman could smell a thief who was 160 kms away
* Vols, a French GSD has cleared 11'9" in high jump
* Bhola Munda of Ranchi was saved from a wild elephant attack by fierce barking of his pet dog
* When VinodKumar, a dog trainer of Chandigarh got married more than a dozen dogs participated in 'Baraat'
* In Columbia, there is a school exclusively for dogs wherein they are even told stories!
* Dogs can recognize blue, yellow and grey colours
* First ever cloned dog is Snuppy. Professor Suk Hwang of South Korea is his chief architect
* A robot dog 'Ibo' is developed to alert obese people against over-eating
* There is an exclusive museum about dogs in USA
* In Kenya a dog saved an abandoned baby by name 'Angel'. The dog was later aptly named as "Camboji" meaning saviour
* Olfactory ability of dogs is 100 million times more than other animals
* Auditory capacity of dogs is five times that of human beings
* 'Kandya', hunting dog owned by Chathrapathi Sahu Maharaj once saved him from a tiger. When the King died, Kandya also gave up his life

---

Bobby, a collie dog got lost in Indiana of USA. It took him six months to reach his hometown at Oregon 3000 miles away

* Leena, an American Foxhound gave birth to 23 puppies in a single litter
* Aristotle believed that Tibetan Mastiff dog is the result of breeding tiger with dog
* According to Egyptian mythology, a dog by name Arubis protects the graves
* Vinod Mehtha, Editor of Outlook Magazine has named his dog 'Editor'
* Scientists at Safar rebirth Research Centre, Pittsburg, have given life to a dead dog. This is the first ever incidence of scientifically recorded rebirth

---

Chacolate, an Argentine dog protected a boy from bee stings but died in the process

Please suggest a sweet name for my pet.

You may choose a nice name for your pet from this list-

ACHILLES
ACTION
ADMIRAL
ADONIS
ADRIATIC
AESOP
AFFINITY
AJAX
AKIRA
ALADDIN
ALASTAIR
ALCATRAZ
ALCHEMY
ALDO
ALEXIA
ALFALFA
ALGER
ALI BABA
ALLEGRO
ALOYSIUS
ALPACA
ALPHA
ALPINE
AMABLE
AMARETTO BAJA
BALBOA
BALDRIC
BALDWIN
BALDY
BALI
BALLERINA
BAM-BAM
BAMBI

BAMBINO
BAMBOOZLER
BANDANNA
BANDIT
BANDITO
BANGLE
BANJO
BANNER
BANQUO
BANSHEE
BANZA!
BARBARIAN
BARBARINO
BARFLY
BARNACLE
BARNEY
BARON
BAROQUE
BART
BARTHOLOMEW
BARTON
BASEL
BASHFUL
BASIL
BASS
BAXTER
BAYOU
BAZOOKA
BEACHBABY
BEACHCOMBER
BEAMER
BEANS
BEAR

BEARLOCK HOLMES
BEAU
BEAUCOUP
BEAUREGARD
BEAUTY
BEDOUIN
BEEFEATER
BEELZEBUB
BEEPER
BEETHOVEN
BEETLEJUICE
BEGONIA
BELLA MIA
BELLADONNA
BELLBOY
BELLE
BELUGA
BEN
BENGAL
BENJI
BENNINGTON
BENTLEY
BEOWOOF
BERBER
BERET
BERTHA
BESSIE
BETA
BETTY BOOP
BEULAH
BEWITCHED
BIALY
BIANCO or BIANCA

Columbus used cruel dogs to threaten the natives of newly found islands

BIDDY (BRIDGET)
BIG BOY
BOZO
BRADSTREET
BRAIN
BRAINCHILD
BRAINDEAD
BRANDO
BRANDY
BRANDYWINE
BRASSY
BRAT
BRATWURST
(BRAUTTY)
BRAVO
BREATHLESS
MAHONEY
BREW
BREWSKY
BRIE
BRIER
BRIT
BRITTANY
BROADWAY
BRONCO
BRONSON
BRONTË
BROUHAHA
BROWN SUGAR
BROWNIE CADILLAC
CAESAR
CAGNEY
CAIRO
CAJUN
CALAMITY
CALIBER
CALICO
CALIFORNIA
CALLOWAY
CALVIN
CALYPSO
CAMELOT
CAMEMBERT
CAMEO
CAMUS
CANDY
CANIS
CAPER
CAPO
CAPONE
CAPRICORN
CAPTAIN
CARAMBA
CARAMEL
CARAMELO
CARGO
CARIBOU
CARNATION
CAROB
CAROLINA
CARRAWAY
CASANOVA
CASBAH DA VINCI
DAGWOOD
DAIQUIRI
DAISY
DAKOTA
DALI
DALLAS
DAMAGE
DAMSEL
DANCER
DANDELION
DANK
DANTE
DANU
DANUBE
DAPHNE
DAREDEVIL
DARTH VADER
DASH
DASHER
DAWN
DAZZLER
DEBUTANTE
DEEOGEE
DEGAS
DÉJÀ VU
DELILAH
DELTA
DERBY
DESDEMONA
DESIREE
DESOTO
DESPERADO
DETONATOR
DETOUR
DEUCE
DEVIL E.T.
EBI
EBONY
ECHO
ECLIPSE
EDELWEISS
EDGE
EGGO
EINSTEIN
ELF
ELIAS
ELMER
ELMO

ELROY
ELSA
ELVIRA
ELVIS
EMERALD
EMERSON
EMILY
EMMA
ENCHILADA
ENERGIZER
ENZO
EPCOT
EPIC
EPSTEIN
EQUITY
ERROL
ESCAPADE
ESCORT
ESKIMO
ESPRIT
ESPRESSO
EUPHRATES
EUREKA
EUROPA
EWOK
EXCALIBUR FALCON
FANCY
FANDANGO
FANG
FANTASIA
FATAL BEAUTY
FATS
FATSO
FATTY
FAUST
FAUX PAS
FEDORA

FELIX
FENDER (BENDER)
FENNEL
FENWAY
FERDINAND
FERREO
FIDO
FIESTA
FIFI
FIGARO
FIJI
FIKRI
FINK
FINN
GAELIC
GALILEO
GAMBLER
GARBO
GARGOYLE
GARLIC
GARP
GATEKEEPER
GATOR
GATSBY
GAVIN
GAZELLE
GAZPACHO
GECKO
GEEKIE
GEEZER
GEISHA
GEMINI
GENESIS
GENGHIS
GENIE
GENIUS
GEORGIA

GEPPETTO
GERBIL
GERONIMO
GERTRUDE
GHIRADELLI
GHOSTBUSTER
GIDDY
GIDEON
GIDGET
GIGGLES
GIGI
GIGOLO
GILLIGAN
GIMP
GIN
GINGER
GINGERSNAP
GINGHAM
GINSENG
GIPPER
GIRL
GIRLFRIEND
GIRO
GISELLE
GIZMO
GLADSTONE
GNOME
GOBBLE
GOBLIN
GODFATHER
GODZILLA
GOETHE
GOLDIE
GOLDILOCKS
GOLIATH
GOMER
GOOBER

Dogs when happy move their tail more to the right and when sad or angry move it more to the left according to a research conducted by Tristy University

GOOCH
GOOMBA
GOOSE
GOPHER
GORDO
GORGEOUS
GORILLA
GORKY
GOUDA
GRACE
GRANDEUR
GRAZIE
GREMLIN
GRETEL
GREYSTOKE
GRITS
GRIZZLY
GROUCHO
GROVER
GRUMPUS
GRUMPY
GRUNGE
GRUNION
GRUNT
GUAYMAS
GUCCI
GUFFAW
GUIDO
GUINEVERE
GULLIVER
GUMBALL
GUMBO
GUMBY
GUMDROP
GUMMIE BEAR
GUMPS
GUNG HO
GUNNER
GUNTHER
GURU
GUS
GUSSY
GUSTO
GUY
GYPSY
GYRO
HACHI-KO
HACKI-SACK
HALCYON
HALEY
HAM
HAMLET
HAMMER
HANCOCK
HANDSOME
HANNIBAL (the Cannibal)
HANSEL
HAPPY
HAPPY FEET
HARD ROCK
HARDY
HARLEY
HARMONY
HARPO
HARVEY
HASKELL
HAVANA
HAVOC
HAWK
HAWKEYE
HAZER
HEARTBREAKER
HEARTS
HEATHCLIFF
HEATHER
HEAVEN
HEDGEHOG
HEFTY
HEIDI
HEIRESS
HERCULES
HERMAN
HERMES
HERMIT
HERO
HERSHEY
HICKORY
HILDA
HIPPO
HIPPODROME
HISTORIA
HOAGIE
HOBBIT
HOBO
HOCUS-POCUS
HOG
HOLLY
HOLLYWOOD
HOMEBOY
HOMER
HOMEY
HONCHO
HONEY
HONEY BEAR
HONEYBEE
HONEYSUCKLE ROSE
HONKY-TONK
HOOCH
HOOD

Ella Vandal of NewYork has willed her property worth 15 million pounds to Toby, a poodle dog

HOOFMAN
HOOK
HOOLIGAN
HOOSIER
HOOVER
HOPE
HORACE
HORATIO
HORS D'OUVRES
HORSHACK
HORUS
HOT DOG
HOTSHOT
HOUDINI
HOWARD
HOWLER
HUBBA HUBBA
HUBBLE
HUCK
HUDSON
HUGGER-MUGGER
HUGO
HULK
HUMDINGER
HUMPHREY
HUNTER
HUNTRESS
HURRICANE
HYDE
ICARUS
ICEMAN
ICE-T
ICON
IDA
IDITAROD
IGGY
IGLOO
IGNATIUS
IGOR
INCA
INDIANA
INDIE
INDIGO
INFINITY
INKY
INTELECTUS
INTREPID
IODINE
IOTA
IRA
IRIE
IRIS
IRRESISTIBLE
ISABELLE
ISHTA
ISHTAR
ISIS
IVY
J.B.
J.F.K.
JABBERWOCKY
JACK DANIEL'S
JACKPOT
JADE
JAG
JAI ALAI
JAILBAIT
JAKE
JALAPEÑO
JAMAICA
JAMES DEAN
JASMINE
JASPER
JAVA
JAZZ
JE T'AIME
JED
JEDI
JEKYLL
JELLY BEAN
JELLY-BELLY
JEMIMA
JERKY
JERSEY
JESSE
JET
JETHRO
JEZEBEL
JIGSAW
JINGLES
JINX
JITTERBUG
JOKER
JOY
JUBILEE
JUDGE
JUGHEAD
JULEP
JULIET
JUMBO
JUNE
JUNIOR
JUNIPER
JUPITER
JUSTUSK.O.
K-9
KAFKA
KAHLUA
KAISER
KALAMAZOO
KALEIDOSCOPE

Fashion shows are conducted now-a-days to launch pet dresses

KANDINSKY
KARMA
KATMANDU
KAYLE
KEEPERS
KELLOGG
KENO
KENTUCKY
KENYA
KERMIT
KEWPIE
KIBBLES
KID
KIELBASA
KIKI
KIKU
KILLER
KILO
KIMBUNDU
KING
KING KONG
KINKO
KIPLING
KISSES
KIWI
KLONDIKE
KLUTZ
KNAIDEL
KNICKERBOCKER
KNOCKOUT
KNUCKLES
KOALA
KOBI
KODA
KOKO
KONA
KOOKABURRA
KOOL
KORBEL
KOSMIC
KOSMO
KRISPY
KRYPTONITE
KUDU
KUJO
KUMA
LABYRINTH
LACEY
LADRON
LADY
LAKER
LAMBCHOP
LAMBORGHINI
LANCELOT
LASER
LASHES
LASSIE
LAVENDER
LAZARUS
LEILA
LEMON
LEO
LEVI
LEXIS
LIABILITY
LIBERTY
LICKUMS
LIEBCHEN
LIGHTNING
LIGHTNING BUG
LILAC
LILITH
LIMBO
LINK
LINUS
LION
LIONHEART
LIPS
LIRA
LISBON
LITMUS
LITTLE BIT
LITTLE GUY
LITTLE ONE
LIZARD
LOBO
LOLA
LOLITA
LOLLY
LOONY
LOTUS
LOVE-BUG
LOVE-PIG
LOVER
LOVERBOY
LOVERGIRL
LOVESONG
LOVEY
LOVEY DOVEY
LUCKY
LUDWIG
LULLABY
LULU
LUNATICMAC
MAC-ATTACK
MACBETH
MACHETE
MACHIAVELLI
MACHO
MACINTOSH
MACKEREL

First dog to act as blindmen's eye was a German Shepherd by name Buddy

MACMILLAN
MAD MAX
MADAME BUTTER-FLY
MADURO
MAESTRO
MAFIOSO
MAGGIE
MAGIC
MAGNA
MAGNET
MAGNOLIA
MAGNUM
MAGPIE
MAHIMAHI
MAHOGANY
MAI TAI
MAILMAN
MAJESTIC
MAJOR
MAKO
MALCOLM
MAMACITA
MAMBA
MAMBO
MAMIE
MANCHU
MANDY
MANHATTAN
MANNERS
MAPLE SYRUP
MARASCHINO
MARAUDER
MARBLE
MARDI GRAS
MARIACHI
MARIE ANTOINETTE
MARIGOLD
MARILYN
MARLBORO
MARLEY
MARMADUKE
MARMALADE
MARQUEE
MARSHMALLOW
MARTIAN
MARTINI
MATADOR
MATILDA
MATISSE
MATOK
MATTIE
MATZO
MAUI
MAVERICK
MAX
MAY
MAYA
MAYHEM
MAYNARD
MAZEL TOV
McCOY
ME TOO
MEADOW
MEATLOAF
MEDEA
MEDUSA
MEE-KROB
MELANGE
MELLOW
MELODY
MELON-HEAD
MELVIN
MENAGE
MERCEDES
MERLIN
MESQUITE
METIS
METRO
MIATA
MICKEY
MIDAS
MIDGET
MIDNIGHT
MIGNON
MILES
MINERVA
MING
MINK
MINNIE
MIRÓ
MISERY
MISHA
MISSIE
MISSING LINK
MISTLETOE
MOCHA
MOET
MOGUL
MOHAVE
MOHAWK
MOHICAN
MO-JO
MOLE
MON AMI
MON CHER or MA CHERIE
MONA
MONA LISA
MONGOOSE
MONK

First ever cloned dog is Snuppy. Professor Suk Hwang of South Korea is his chief architect

MONKEY
MONTEGO
MONTY
MOOCHY
MOODY
MOONBEAM
MOONDANCE
MOONGODDESS
MOONMIST
MOONRAKER
MOONSHINE
MOONSTRUCK
MOOSE
MOPSY
MOPTOP
MORK
MOROCCO
MORRIS
MORTIMER
MOSELLE
MOUSTACHE
MOUTON
MOVADO
MOXIE
MOZART
MU SHU
MUDD
MUDDLES
MUDPIE
MUENSTER
MUFFIN
MUG
MUGSY
MULBERRY
MUMBLES
MUNCHER
MUNCHKIN
MUNCHYKIN
MUSE
MUSTANG
MUTANT
MUTT
MYSTIC
MYTH
NACHO
NAIROBI
NAPA
NAPOLEON
NAPPY
NAVAJO
NAVAR
NAVIGATOR
NELLIE
NEON
NEPTUNE
NEUTRON
NEWSPRINT
NEWT
NEWTON
NIBBLES
NICKLEBY
NICKLES
NIETZSCHE
NIFTY
NIGHTMARE
NIKE
NIKITA
NIKO
NINA
NINJA
NIPPER
NISSAN
NISTKA
NITRO
NOAH
NOEL
NOISEMAKER
NOISETTE
NOMAD
NOSFERATU
NOVA
NOVELLA
NUDGE
NUDNIK
NUGGET
NUTMEG
NYMPHO.J.
O.T.M.
OBERON
ODYSSEY
OINK
OKIE
OKRA
OL' SPORT
OLD YELLER
OLIVER
OLLIE
OMEGA
ONOMATOPOEIA
ONYX
OOGA-BOOGA
OPAL
OPHELIA
ORBIT
OREO
ORION
ORPHAN ANNIE
OSCAR
OTHELLO
OTIS
OTTO

Grey hounds can run at a speed of 70 kms per hour

OUIJA
OUTLAW
OUTRIGGER
OUZO
OX
OZ
OZONE
OZZIE
PACHYDERM
PACO
PADDINGTON
PADDY
PADUA
PAGAN
PAGODA
PAISLEY
PAL
PALOMA
PALOMINO
PANACHE
PANAMA
PANDA
PANDEMONIUM
PANDORA
PANSY
PANTHER
PAPILLON
PAPOOSE
PAPRIKA
PAPU
PAPYRUS
PARADISE
PARAGON
PARIS
PATCHES
PÂTÉ
PATHFINDER
PATRIOT
PATSY
PATTON
PAUPER
PAVLOV
PAWS
PAZZO
PEABODY
PEACHES
PEANUTS
PEASEBLOSSOM
PEBBLES
PEEWEE
PENELOPE
PENN
PENNE
PEPE
PEPPER
PEPPERMINT
PERITAR
PERIWINKLE
PERNOD
PERRO
PERSEPHONE
PERSEUS
PESO
PEST
PETIT ANGE
PETRA
PETRARCH
PETULIA
PETUNIA
PEUGEOT
PEYOTE
PHANTOM
PHARAOH
PHAROS
PHOENIX
PIAZZA
PICASSO
PICCOLO
PICKLES
PICKWICK
PIEDMONT
PIGGLES-WIGGLES
PIGGY
PIGGY-WIGGY
PING
PINKY
PINOCCHIO
PINTO
PIPER
PIPPI
PIRANHA
PIRATE
PIROUETTE
PISCES
PISTOL
PISTON
PIT-STOP
PITTER-PATTER
PIZZAZZ
PLATO
PLATTY (PLATYPUS)
PLAYGIRL
PLUTO
POCO
POET
POGO
POINDEXTER
POKERFACE
POLITIX
POLLY
POLO

Hitler killed his dog Blondy so that it will not be adopted by non-Aryans

POLTERGEIST
POM-POM
PONG
PONGO
POOCH
POOH
POOH-BAH
POOKIE
POP
POPEYE
PORKCHOP
PORKER
PORSCHE
PORTIA
PORTLY
POTPOURRI
POUILLY-FUISSÉ
PRANCER
PRECIOUS
PRESIDENT
PRESTO
PRETTI
PAWSPRETTY
PRETTY BABY
PRETZEL
PRIMA DONNA
PRIMO
PRINCE or PRIN-CESS
PRISSY
PRODIGY
PROFESSOR
PROTON
PRUDENCE
PUCK
PUDDING
PUDDLES
PUDGE
PUDGETTE
PUFF
PUFFBALL
PUGNOSE
PUMPKIN
PUNCH
PUNK
PUPA
PUPPY
PUTT-PUTT
PYGMYQANTAS
QUASI
QUASIMODO
QUEEN BEE
QUEENY
QUICHE
QUICK
QUICKSILVER
QUINCY
QUIRK
QUIXOTERADAR
RAGDOLL
RAGE
RAGGEDY ANN
RAGING BULL
RAGMOP
RAGS
RAGTIME
RAGU
RAIDER
RAIN
RAINBOW
RAISIN
RAJAH
RALPH
RAMBO
RANGER
RASCAL
RASSELAS
RASTA
RAVEL
RAVEN
RAWHIDE
RAY
RAZZ
RAZZMATAZZ
REBEL
RED or REDHEAD
REDBEARD
REEBOK
REEF
REGALO
REM
REMINGTON
REMY
RENEGADE
RENO
REPO
REUBEN
REX
RHAPSODY
RHEA
RHETT
RHINESTONE
RHINO
RHODES
RHONE
RICHES
RICKY-TICKY-TAVI
RICOCHET
RICOTTA
RIDER
RIFFRAFF

In Columbia, there is a school exclusively for dogs wherein they are even told stories!

RIN TIN TIN
RINGLEADER
RINGO
RIO
RIP VAN WINKLE
RIPLEY
RIPPLE
RITZ or RITZY
ROACH
ROB ROY
ROCCA
ROCK
ROCKER
ROCKET
ROCKO or ROCKY
ROCOCO
RODEO
ROGAN
ROGUE
ROJO
ROLLS
ROMA
ROMEO
ROMULUS
RONDEAU
ROO (KANGAROO)
ROOKIE
ROOSTER
ROOT BEER
ROSARITA
ROSCOE
ROSEBUD
ROSIE
ROT
ROTHSCHILD
ROTTEN
ROVER

ROWDY
ROXANNE
ROXY
ROYAL
.RUBY
RUFF
RUFFIAN
RUFFLES
RUFUS
RUGRAT
RUMPELSTILTSKIN
RUNNER
RUNT
RUPERT
RUSTY
SABBATH
SABER
SABER-TOOTH
SABLE
SADIE
SAFARI
SAFFRON
SAGA
SAGE
SAHARA
SAILOR
SAKE
SALAMANDER
(MANDY)
SALSA
SALTY
SALVATORE
SAM
SAMBUCA
SAM-I-AM
SAMMY
SAMSON

SAMURAI
SAND RAT
SANDMAN
SANGRIA
SANTA FE
SANTINI
SANTO
SAPPHIRE
SARASOTA
SARGE
SASHA
SASHIMI
SASQUATCH
SASSAFRAS
SASSY
SATAY
SATCHMO
SATIN
SAUCE or SAUCY
SAUSAGE
SAVAGE
SAVANNAH
SAVERNAKE
SAVOY
SCAMPER
SCAMPI
SCARBOROUGH
SCARLET
SCHATZE
SCHMOO
SCHMOOZE
SCHNAPPS
SCHNOOK
SCHOONER
SCHWARZKOPF
SCHWEPPES
SCINTILLA

In Kenya a dog saved an abandoned baby by name 'Angel'. The dog was later aptly named as "Camboji" meaning saviour

SCOOBIE
SCOOTER
SCORPIO
SCOTCH
SCOUNDREL
SCOUT
SCRAPPY
SCRAPPY TOO
SCROOGE
SCRUFFY
SCRUMPTIOUS
SCUBA
SCUD
SCYLLA
SEA DOG
SEABREEZE
SEAL
SENECA
SERA
SERENADE
SERENDIPITY
SERENGETI
SERGEANT
SEUSS
SEYCHELLES
SEYMOUR
SHADOW
SHAH
SHAKESPEARE
SHALIMAR
SHAMROCK
SHAMU
SHANE
SHANGRI-LA
SHARKEY
SHARP
SHAWNEE
SHEBA
SHE-DEVIL
SHEER
SHEIK
SHELLEY
SHENANIGANS
SHERIFF
SHERLOCK
SHERWOOD
SHIITAKE
SHIKSA
SHIM SHIM SHIREE
SHIVA
SHOELESS
SHOGUN
SHOOTER
SHORTY, SHORT-
CAKE or
SHORTSTACK
SHOTGUN
SHOWBOAT
SHOWOFF
SHRAMSBERG
SHRAPNEL
SHREDDER
SHRIMP
SHYLOCK
SICILIANO
SIDEWAYS
SIDNEY
SIEGFRIED
SIENNA
SIERRA
SIGMUND
SILHOUETTE
SILKY
SILVER
SILVERSPOON
SIMPLY RED
SIN
SINATRA
SINBAD
SINCLAIR
SINGER
SISSY
SITTING BULL
SIX TOES
SKEDADDLE
SKEEDER
SKIDDER
SKIPPER
SKIPPY
SKITTLES
SKY
SKY HAWK
SKYROCKET
SKYWALKER
SLATE
SLEESTACK
SLICKER
SLIPPERS
SLOBBER-PUSS
SLOTH
SLUGGER
SLY
SMASHER
SMOKEY
SMOOCHER
SMORES
SNAGGLETOOTH
SNAKER
SNAP
SNARL
SNEAKERS

Leena, an American Foxhound gave birth to 23 puppies in a single litter

SNEEZY
SNICKERS
SNIFFER
SNIFFLES
SNIFTER
SNOCAP
SNOOGYBEAR
SNOOKER
SNOOKS
SNOOKUMS
SNOOPER
SNOOPY
SNOOTY
SNO-PEA
SNORTER
SNOW, SNOWBALL or SNOWFLAKE
SNOWBERRY
SNOWBUNNY
SNOWMAN
SNUFFLES
SNUGGLES or SNUGGLE-PUSS
SOCKS
SOCRATES
SOLEIL
SOLO
SOLOMON
SOLSTICE
SONATA
SOONER
SOPHIE
SORBET
SORCERER or SORCERESS
SOUEEE
SOURDOUGH
SOUTHERN COMFORT
SOUTHPAW
SPADES
SPAGHETTI
SPAGO
SPAM
SPANKY
SPARKEY or SPARKLE
SPARKPLUG
SPARROW
SPECS
SPEEDY
SPELLBINDER
SPHINX
SPICY
SPIDER
SPIKE
SPINNER
SPIRIT
SPITFIRE
SPLASH
SPOCK
SPOOKY
SPORT
SPOT
SPRITE
SPUDS
SPUMANTI
SPUNKY
SPUTNIK
SPY
SPYRO
SQUAT
SQUEAKY
SQUID
SQUIRT
STAR
STARDUST or STARLIGHT
STARGAZER
STARLET
STELLA
STELLAR
STERLING
STETSON
STING
STINKER or STINKER BELLE
STINKY
STOLI
STONEY
STORM or STORMY
STOWAWAY
STRAY
STREGA
STRUDEL
STUBBY or STUBBLES
STUMP
SUGAR
SUGARBABY
SUGARBAKER
SUGAR-PLUM
SUKIYAKI
SULFUR
SULTAN
SUMO
SUNDANCE
SUNDOWN
SUNI
SUNKISS
SUNNYBROOK

Many major metros of the world have 5 star hotels for dogs

SUNRISE
SUNSHINE
SUPERTRAMP
SUSHI
SUSSUDIO
SWAMI
SWAMPY
SWEATHOG
SWEET CHEEKS
SWEET PEA
SWEETHEART,
SWEETIE or SWEET-
NESS
SWIZZLE
SYMPHONY
SYNERGY
T.L.C.
T.N.T.
TABOO
TABRIZ
TAFFY
TAG
TAHITI
TALAHACHE
TALISMAN
TALLYHO
TAMAHTO
TAMARA
TAMPEST
TANG
TANGO
TANK
TANKA
TANNER
TAO
TAOS
TAR
TARA
TARGA
TARO
TAROT
TARRAGON
TARTINE
TARTUFFE
TARZAN
TATTERS
TATTLETALE
TATTOO
TAURUS
TAUSKEY
TAXI
TAZ
TAZER
T-BONE
TEACUP
TEAL
TEASE or TEASER
TENNESSEE
TEQUILA
TERMINATOR
TERRA-COTTA
TERROR
TESS
TESTAROSSA
TEXAS
THAI
THATCHER
THOR
THORN or THISTLE
THUDPAW
THUMPER
THUNDER
THYME
TIAMO
TIARA
TIE-DYE
TIGER
TIGGER
TILLY
TINKER
TINKERBELL
TINKERTOY
TINKLE BELL
TINMAN
TINSEL
TINY
TIPSY
TISSOT
TITAN
TITIAN
TIZZY or TIZZ
TOAD
TOBY
TOFU
TOMAHAWK
TOMBA
TOM-TOM
TONTO
TOOTER
TOOTSIE
TOPAZ
TOREADOR
TORNADO
TORO
TORTS
TOTO
TOUCHÉ
TOVA
TOYBOX
TRAILBLAZER
TRAMP

TREAT
TREKKY
TRICKY
TRILOGY
TRINKET
TRIP
TRIXIE
TROJAN
TROLL
TROPICANA
TROUBADOUR
TROUBLE
TROUPER
TROUT
TRUFFAUT
TRUFFLEHUNTER
TRUFFLES
TRUMP
TRURMAN
TRYST
TSUNAMI
TUBBO (also TUBBY or TUBS)
TUFFYTUGBOAT
TULIP
TUMBLEWEED
TUNA
TUNDRA
TURBO
TURKEY
TUTTI-FRUTTI
TUTU
TWEETY
TWERP
TWINKIE
TWINKLE
TWISTER
TYCOON
TYPHOON
UDO
UFO
UGLY-BUGLY
ULYSSES
ULANOVA
UMA
UMPA LUMPA
UNAGI
UNCLE SAM
URANUS
URCHIN
URIEL
URSA
URSULA
USHKI
UTOPIA VACA
VAGABOND
VALENTINE
VALENTINO
VAN GOGH
VAN-DAMME
VANILLA
VAQUERO
VEGGIE
VELCRO
VELVET
VENUS
VENUS DE MILO
VERONA
VICHYSSOISE
VIOLET
VIPER
VISA
VIVA
VIXEN
VOLTAIRE
VOODOO
VOYAGER
VROOM VROOM
WACKY
WADDLES
WAG-A-LOT
WAGS
WALDO
WALLFLOWER
WALRUS
WANDA
WARHOL
WARLOCK
WARRIOR
WARTHOG
WASABE
WEB
WELLINGTON
WHIRLWIND
WHISKEY
WHISPER or WHISPERWIND
WHOOPIE
WIGGLES
WILBUR
WILD THING
WILDWOOD
WILFRED
WILHELMINA
WILLOUGHBY
WILLOW
WILSON
WIMPY
WINDJAMMER
WINDSOR
WINDY

Savar, a Doberman could smell a thief who was 160 kms away

WINK
WINSTON
WINTHROP
WISEGUY
WITCH
WIZARD
WIZKID
WOLFGANG
WONDERDOG
WONTON
WOODSTOCK
WOODWIND
WOODY
WOOF
WOOKIE
WOOLY MAMMOTH
WRANGLER
WRIGLEY
XANADU
XANTHUS
XAVIER
XENA
XEROX
XERXESYABBA-
DABBA-DOO
YAHOO
YAMASEE
YANKEE
YAYA
YEAGER
YODA
YOGI BEAR
YORGY
YOSEMITE
YOU TOO
YO-YO
YUKON
YULE
YUMA
YUMMY
ZACK
ZAIRE
ZEBU
ZEKE
ZELDA
ZELIG
ZEPELLIN
ZEPHYR
ZEPPO
ZERO
ZEUS
ZIGGY
ZIPPITY DO DA
ZODIAC
ZOE
ZOMBIE
ZOOEY
ZOOM ZOOM
ZOPPICO
ZORRO
ZSA ZSA
ZULU
ZUNI

Scientists at Safar rebirth Research Centre, Pittsburg, have given life to a dead dog. This is the first ever incidence of scientifically recorded rebirth

Afgan Hound

Basset Hound

Beagle

Blood Hound

Bordeaux

Borzoi

Boxer

Bull dog

Bull Mastiff

Collie

Bull Terrier

Dachshund

Chihuahua

Dalmation

Cocker Spaniel

Doberman

English Mastiff

Great Dane

German Shepherd

Grey Hound

German Spitz

Irish Setter

Golden Retriever

Labrador Retriever

Lhasa Apso

Pug

Mudhol Hound

Rajapalyam

Pomeranian

Rottweiler

Saluki

Shar Pie

St. Bernard

Shi Tzu

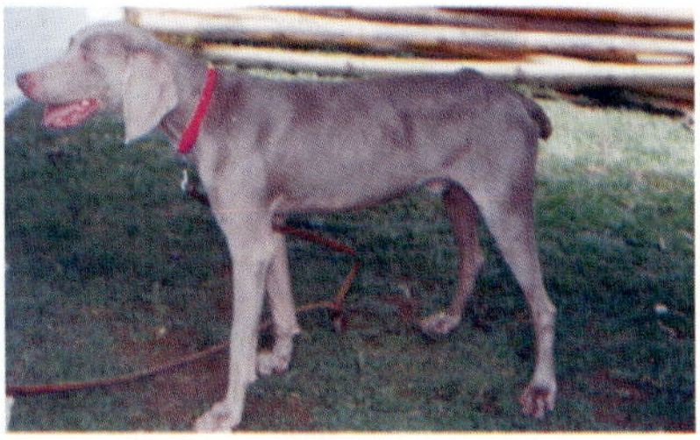

Weimeraner

Welsh Corgi

Index